I DON'T WANT TO BE UNDERSTOOD

I DON'T WANT TO BE UNDERSTOOD

JOSHUA JENNIFER ESPINOZA

Alice James Books
NEW GLOUCESTER, MAINE
alicejamesbooks.org

10 9 8 7 6 5 4 3 2 1

Alice James Books are published by Alice James Poetry Cooperative, Inc.

Alice James Books
Auburn Hall
60 Pineland Drive, Suite 206
New Gloucester, ME 04260
www.alicejamesbooks.org

Library of Congress Cataloging-in-Publication Data

Names: Espinoza, Joshua Jennifer, 1987- author.
Title: I don't want to be understood / Joshua Jennifer Espinoza.
Other titles: I do not want to be understood
Description: New Gloucester, ME : Alice James Books, 2024.
Identifiers: LCCN 2024006540 (print) | LCCN 2024006541 (ebook) | ISBN
  9781949944631 (trade paperback) | ISBN 9781949944358 (epub)
Subjects: LCGFT: Poetry.
Classification: LCC PS3605.S634 I33 2024 (print) | LCC PS3605.S634
  (ebook) | DDC 811/.54--dc23/eng/20240216
LC record available at https://lccn.loc.gov/2024006540
LC ebook record available at https://lccn.loc.gov/2024006541

Alice James Books gratefully acknowledges support from individual donors, private foundations,
and the National Endowment for the Arts.

Cover image: Pink Table by Sara Regal - www.sararegal.com

CONTENTS

1   VIOLENCE IS THE SCROLL UPON WHICH HER HISTORY IS RECORDED

Airport Ritual	1
Every Day	3
Personal Statement	5
Every Morning I Walk through a Field	7
Makeup Ritual	8
Questions for Your Admirer	9
The Heat Death of the Universe	10
The Threat	11
As He Killed Me I Imagined Him	12
I Want to Write a Poem	13
Return to Light	14
Warm	15
Birthday Suits	16
Coming Out	18
To My Parents	20
Snow	22
Particulate Matter	24
My Freedom	25
My Name—	26
Trans Woman's First Rental Application	27

Queering Success 28

You're Going to Die Today 29

Poem 30

The Blueness of the Room 31

The Front Door 32

Game Animal 33

Justification 34

Time-Lapse Video of Trans Woman Collapsing Inward
    like a Dying Star 35

Gangrenous Love 37

How Many Colors There Are vs. How Many Colors Have Been Named 38

2   AND THEN CAME THE NAMING

Newsfeed 41

Poem 42

Housewife from Planet X 43

Poem 47

Coercion Road 48

A Confession 49

A Confession 50

Childhood Prayer 52

Espinoza: 53

Poem 54

Resurrection 55

Loss Ritual 56

Airport Ritual 57

Normal 59

Real Woman 60

Where and What I Am 61

We 62

How I Make a Poem 63

Your Weakness 64

Today I Was Alone 66

I Talked to That Spirit Again 67

This Is What Makes Us Worlds   68

Memoir   69

The Present   70

By the Cemetery on Pine   72

Biography of a Snowstorm   73

Addendum   74

Departure   75

It Doesn't Matter If I'm Understood   78

ONE

VIOLENCE

IS THE

SCROLL

UPON WHICH

HER HISTORY

IS RECORDED

AIRPORT RITUAL

The following is a true story:

An anomaly is spotted. A woman is taken aside.

I am going to have to touch you now, an agent says. *I am going to use the front of my hands on most of you, and the back of my hands on your private parts. Is there anything you need to let me know before I proceed?*

I'm trans, the woman leans in to whisper, unsure if she means this as a warning or an apology.

That's okay, the agent says as she grabs the woman's shoes. *Would you like to take this elsewhere?*

Before the woman can answer, the thing in her pants that set the sensors off suddenly expands, tearing through her clothes and revealing an amorphous blob of cosmic energy. It is purplish and void-colored at the same time. There is an impossible shimmer to it. It grows outward, enveloping the agent, the body-scanning machine, and the white dads in red baseball hats gawking at her predicament.

Then the whole terminal. Then the entire airport.

The military plans a strike in response. Some trans guy who fought for the right to kill people on behalf of an empire that hates him is chosen to operate the drone. Better optics, someone thought.

When hit, the woman grows hundreds of times her size. The city of Irvine is pretty much toast. Fox News is floating the idea of forcing trans people into detention facilities: *Until we're sure they don't all pose the threat of having expanding cosmic blobs for genitalia.* It's polling well. Meanwhile,

the woman at the center of the plasma or whatever-the-fuck-it-is
just wants someone to say one thing to her
that doesn't feel like kite string wrapped around an open wound
in a warm, strong wind. But it doesn't happen.

So, she sings something to herself.

A song she heard in a grocery store once.

Michelle Branch. Frozen food aisle. Instant tears.

She remembers her life, floats up into a cloud, gets carried away.

No one can track her. She is dispersed, rained down upon the dirt and patchy grass where her old house used to be. Flowers bloom. People pluck them and give them to people they love.

Everything is normal.

EVERY DAY

You'll feel fear as a blue sky.
A green light. A line of people
swaying in place like grass.
One is always emerging
into something.
Out of something else.
You've traveled by light
to get here.
Each panic attack
had its own frequency.
You memorized the language.
It barely touches you now.
All you've lost is blood,
your old home,
bits of who you used to be
embedded in stucco.
Every day was ordinary.
You'd wake up and pretend
to be a boy.
You'd go to sleep and dream
of being a woman.
Eventually you never
regained consciousness.
This wasn't a decision.
It's just what happens
when you realize
how far away stars are.
How old the universe is.
How a life is an open thing
leaking out into
the air around it.
You are afraid of being seen.
You are afraid of being named.
Even as you flow from

street to street
wrapped in dead roses
you'll remember who lives here.
You can't wait to be able
to say no to all of them.

PERSONAL STATEMENT

I don't believe I was born, maybe emerged
from a soupy formation of gays

and other wild things instead. I've gone
on and on telling you all about how I

created myself, took a photograph of what
I was given, tore it up, set it on fire, inhaled

its smoke and grew twenty times my size.
All of this has been said. Today I want to make

this space my own and project my light through
every surface. I think by now I've earned this—

what with the breathing exercises just to leave
the house, and the hyperawareness of every blade

of grass's movement, and the drinking, and the
getting high each night to stave off the nightmares.

You know, just girly things. So here's what you need
to understand—any time I'm doing something I'm doing

something I'm afraid of. This makes each experience
seem new and old at the same time. I'm always like

I don't give a fuck when in reality I am literally
going to die from how much of a fuck I give. Also

I'm a witch and I get all my powers from the wind.
Wow. Aren't I special? Don't you want to love me

with all of your heart for the next ten seconds?

Don't you want to rescue me

from all the things that make you feel safe?

EVERY MORNING I WALK THROUGH A FIELD

Every morning I walk through a field in my head
and I pick the weeds, water the flowers, scatter seeds,

set the trash heap on fire. I never speak a word—never
once do I have to hear the sound of my own voice, and

it is heaven, the blessing of erasure, the harmless
ego death extending far into the woods I dare not

explore. I am a light in the form of a girl, my strong
hands caressing my weak arms. I am my own warm

bath at the end of the day. I come home to myself
and practice breathing. It does not always go so

well and there are times I'd rather be the sky, be
the clouds, be the end of the storm dissipating

over open waters. This unique trans loneliness eats away
at me. It is always at hand, always coming, always

hungry for more of me. No one asks how they can
help and it's fine. I have my flowers. I have my

heap. I have the parts of my body that still belong
to me. I have the will to keep moving.

MAKEUP RITUAL

This is not another feminist poem
about the tyranny of Western standards
of beauty. Or maybe it is.
As a trans woman, I'm still not sure what
I'm allowed to contribute to the topic.
According to some I exist only to
reinforce gendered violence—
my body a blade sliding up and down
the legs of real women
forcing its way under their arms
and carving the language of misogyny
into every surface.
Wow. Who knew I had so much power?
I don't even leave the house unless
I've had time to build a world on my face
and make myself palatable
for public consumption.
Is it so wrong to be afraid
when I've seen what can happen?
When I've had it happen to me?
In my life there is nothing more beautiful
than dissociating in front of a mirror
and drawing perfect lines
across the flesh, wrinkle to wrinkle,
eyes rolling up into themselves,
plastic pulling lashes into little curls.
I live to cover my shadow with blood.
To cake my entire image.
For me, this means something like safety.
Like a hit of oxygen from a falling plane.
The first time I saw my face made-up
I couldn't help but cry it all off.
What will I call myself now? I wondered.
It helps to have a name even though
a name is a room you can never leave.

QUESTIONS FOR YOUR ADMIRER

Who are you and why have you come here / Do you know me / Why are you touching me / Do you want / Me or are you here to end / Me / Take a seat don't bother asking / Notice the softness of my neck / I've been waiting for someone's teeth / To explain to me who I am / Are you hungry or / Can I get you some water / I can open my mouth and give you / Water if it would make you happy / But you want something redder / Something thicker / Something less eager to become air when spilled / You think this is the only way / To get to know me / Why do you want this / I am so unlike what is in me / What is in me knows nothing about me / Go outside and talk to the sidewalk / Press your tongue / To the round spots of flattened gum / Taste what it is to be public-bodied / Ask the palm tree on the corner what she thinks of my predicament / What she'd do in my soft-heavy boots / Let the lamppost talk to you about last night's dream of men's hands reaching / For me / Reach your hand / To the broken glass in the road / And know me

THE HEAT DEATH OF THE UNIVERSE

On an ordinary night I read
comments full of people
saying trans women deserve
to be murdered for existing
and then I brush my teeth and
go to bed like it's nothing.
I sit there and stare
at the ceiling until my eyes
adjust enough to see
the tiny cracks in it.
Good shit, I think to myself.
Great stuff. I have five hundred
names and all of them are bad.
Together they sound like
baseball bats against bone
like wings beating frantically
in an airless space
like God asking herself
if she really exists.
It is surreal to imagine
how I will keep living like this
how I probably won't drink
myself to death
how my skin will stretch
and fold in on itself
like time and space
and memory and dreams
how I would stay alive forever
and suffer the fate of the sun
and the heat death of the universe
just to spite everyone.

THE THREAT

The threat was always implicit.
The man said our hands were alike
and that was why I should be

the same as him—I shuddered in place
beneath the skylight and reached
up to no avail. There were pieces

of me that made sense
as long as they remained in pieces.
There were days I blacked

my eyes and drew blood
on my fingers
just to highlight the difference

between a name and a body
or a body and a soul.
The man saw this and laughed

a nervous laughter.
By the time he finished killing
me I had become something new.

AS HE KILLED ME I IMAGINED HIM

As he killed me I imagined him
floating through the years of his life,
pantomiming violence, eating flowers

bound in fleshy vines, a forest unto
himself. I couldn't help but feel
each moment as my own—

voiceless fists swinging at invisible walls
housing the truth of a manhood
composed by exclusion, a saddening love,

emptied and unfeeling,
drawn helplessly to its roots, wondering
what in this future can be spared.

He says *lightbeams* and *God* and *spirit-
tongued mystery* into my darkness
but the darkness fights back, thrusts itself

into every space of empathy—my softly
beating curse. Once I cried for the smell
of grass, its blood filling the air,

my knees stained green with the world.
Now I drift around, listen to the pain of things,
don't allow my ghost to hurt anyone.

I WANT TO WRITE A POEM

I want to write a poem
about wasting the day
and holding sunlight
in my hands and kissing
the shadows of the dying
trees in my garden.
I want to say something
about the way you looked
the other day in the kitchen
when you spoke a truth
and cried on the floor
next to the oven.
I want to forget I am this
woman in this world
whose eyes are trained
to look for any chance
of violence—how a face
is a landscape and then
becomes a graveyard.
How small confusions
threaten to end me.
I want to enjoy the grass
beneath my feet and sing
songs to it and run my
fingers through the soil and
pray to the beautiful sky.
I want to feel myself
becoming the earth's
dream girl. I want to
be allowed to do this while
I still can.

RETURN TO LIGHT

I don't need to tell you about
the missing time or

the way a mind erases
pages of life to protect itself.

There is no need
to prolong the invisible

and spill buckets of truth
when all we want is a

drop of understanding.
The word *trauma* is dense

like a collapsed sun. You
can hardly see it

as it spins you in place and
reminds you to forget its presence.

When you stand in front of the mirror
and draw a perfect wing above your eye,

you transcend godlessness.
A light appears and makes you promise

not to tell anyone her name.
She says it is important to overemphasize

small victories, like waking up, breathing,
moving through the thick danger of the world.

She says if we do this we might even stay alive
long enough to remember ourselves.

WARM

Warm come back and grip me.
It's been years since I felt you.

I left my family to become a woman
and stopped listening to their voicemails

in order to find you again.
You were a dream I had

twenty years ago:
undressing in an empty room

a soundless chamber
no mirrors, no cameras, no communion

      just flesh
      and bone

   and eye
   and mouth.

In this place I can feel myself.
I can breathe and no one slaps me.

I tap my fingers and no one screams.
I am the girl, the nothing song

who builds herself from scratch
and feels everything.

BIRTHDAY SUITS

I turned twenty-four and
dad decided to take
another stab at making
a man out of me.
On his command, I drove us
out to Hollywood where
you could get three sets of suits
for a hundred bucks.
What a steal! he exclaimed
as though his enthusiasm
would fertilize
something that never
existed within me.
Regardless, I followed him
into the outlet and I
allowed him to wrap
the cheap, heavy thread
around my tired shoulders,
to salt the wound of my body
with his idea of truth.
I let it happen
but I did not forget
what I was
beneath the cover of the flesh:

        five million faggy mountains
        slicing through fields full
        of dreamed-up tongues and
        unnamable bluish grasses
        each blade the length
        of a universe
        stretching inward toward
        a singular point
        of
        life-sustaining unlogic—

dressing myself behind
the heavy polyester curtain,
I listened
as dad held the suit guy hostage
with the oft-told tale
of the night he encountered
real-life, biblical demons,
how at first he felt their presence
tightening inside his chest,
and then witnessed them crawling
up and down his walls
and how he prayed and cursed them
in the name of the Lord
until they dissolved
like sugar into the dark

And he never said this, but I
knew he was convinced they
came for me next

    and colored my nails
    and stretched out my hair
    and adorned me with flowers
    and forced my inside places to whisper
      woman   *woman*   *woman*
    late each night at the
    moment just   before sleep

And I knew he knew
who I was becoming
and I understood
what the suits were for   So

I tossed them in the back
of my trunk
where they sat
waiting for years
and the day I sold that car off
    those suits were still in there

COMING OUT

I wrote a letter. I started drinking
and I didn't stop drinking until
one week ago. I remembered all the fires

that used to threaten our house.
How we'd have to pack up and leave
and hope we'd be returning

to something other than ash.
How you'd pray.
How I'd tell myself God would do whatever

she wanted and we'd just have to deal.
I don't think God would like
what you've done with her.

She was a dream at the beginning of time
who never could have imagined
all this blood.

All these names for things.
All these bodies trying to forget themselves.
I told you how I wanted to die

before this happened.
This earth was always too small
for the sound I make.

You said there were answers in prayer
and you were right.
When I inhale I am praying.

When I get dressed I am praying.
When I climb the mountain and let the wind
fuck me up I am praying.

When I call myself a woman I am praying.

When I cut loose every inch of hell

that was woven through my body I am praying.

TO MY PARENTS

I was a crumb beneath the couch.

I was a ghost.

I was a girl with plans.

I was my head against the tile in front of the fireplace.

I was the mantle above the fireplace, the one that held our portrait.

I was the frame around the photograph, but not the photograph.

I was not the photograph.

I was a boy's skeleton buried beneath the backyard sprinkler.

I was a maggot in the dog's leg after months of neglect.

I was scratching at the garage door, begging to be allowed inside.

I was piss on the roof of the house dripping down the sliding glass door.

I was the water that washed the piss away.

I was mildew smell from soaked bedroom carpet.

I was weeks of quiet waiting for help.

I was the crack in the closet where I punched.

I was the hole in my door someone kicked.

I was the broken lamp somebody else threw.

I was the open purse.

I was the predawn prayer ritual.

I was the cold of the mountain seeping into the house.

I was the wind that took the fences down every fall.

I was the yearly wildfire that always sent us packing.

I was the miracle snow that came once a decade and blessed every surface
with the briefest, thinnest layer of itself before disappearing.

I was the giant lump of glowing night sky that fell behind the mountain,
a sight only I witnessed.

I was the thing nobody believed me about.

I was the tree growing horizontal in our front yard we would run across
first thing after opening the front door.

I was the family of bees that would fill the tree every spring.

I was a pile of lawn clippings.

I was hot soda on a tired lip.

I was hated and inescapable.

I was a reminder of all those inside things you try to drown in the quiet dark of
a cul-de-sac at the very end of a dream.

SNOW

She climbed up the stairs and sat hunched and shivering at the top of the

case, waiting to hear the front door slam. As soon as it did, she ran to her

bedroom placed two pillows beneath her comforter long-ways, spritzed

herself with her favorite perfume, and climbed out of her bedroom

window. The night air was neither warm nor cool against

her speeding body. She had left behind her air-conditioned home

and was now floating through the room temperature of the world. She

imagined his car pulling up beside her could still hear his voice

as it moved in and shoved aside even the sound of the wind, its tone

wrapping around her face like heavy hands shouting, *WHAT DO YOU*

THINK YOU ARE DOING, YOUNG MAN. She wondered what

would happen if she continued running—would his words hold her in

place, her feet frantically peddling inches above the ground, a cartoon

of a woman? Or will his question stretch like rubber, allowing her

to propel herself just out of his reach before her escape

energy betrays her? Will her desire once again become indistinguishable

from anyone else's? No. His words are only in her head. From there, they travel elsewhere.   Into her hands, the way they   shake   when she

reaches for door   handles. Into her   knees, how they   lock themselves   and

melt the keys   for extra locks.   Into the way she   gets close to   people and

then   freezes, kills   communication, dreams   of everything she says rippling

outward   redly.   How her own voice   shoves her away.   How his words

radiated   waves   that made   her entire universe   sound,   look,   feel,

smell,   and taste   like   static,   electric   noise, snow.

PARTICULATE MATTER

I am not allowed to be who I am.

I search for a trace of self
and find nothing.

I am tempted to settle on the first time I wore lipstick.

I was standing on a balcony in front of a bruise-colored tree.

The moon was screaming.

No. I was screaming.

I had to wipe the red from my face and go back home where calling myself a woman was the same as trying to hold my breath at the bottom of a swimming pool.

I have never existed.   I have tried very hard to exist.

If this planet were a forest fire
I would be the smoke drifting off
into the night.

MY FREEDOM

I have choices.

    I can stay

Or go

    By another name

If I have

    Enough time.

I can cross the street

    Or lie down in the middle of it.

I can sell my labor

    Or die.

I can call myself a woman

    Or finally find the right words.

I can make magic

    And continue to stumble over feeding myself.

I can build a new life from nothing

    And still end up with nothing.

MY NAME—

I ask nicely for it.
There is a judge; of course there is.

The room is an orange gas lamp
full of bodies petitioning for

I don't know what.
All I know is I've got

all the proper forms
stapled to my shoulders

and the will to do
whatever it takes to be.

When my time has come,
I drift up and out of my seat.

The man says, *Jennifer*, and
it's like suddenly I exist.

Later, in wet morning air,
I am floating exactly

two inches off
the ground. It feels as though

a tiny gust
could undo everything.

TRANS WOMAN'S FIRST RENTAL APPLICATION

For most of my life, I existed between galaxies.

      It was cold and empty and I forgot about matter.

I could not imagine a thing. So, I

      invented a world from nothing and lived inside it.

I would tell you more about it, but it cannot be written or spoken.

      Instead, I would like you to touch my bleeding neck.

Go on, please. Work

      your fingers into my wound for your comfort.

Find a perfect-feeling space

      inside me, and stay there.

Tell me what you know about me.

      How hard I worked to get here.

How this makes me worthy.

      Let me know what you want to know

so I can be who I need to be.

      Forgive me the bad credit, the years spent in bed,

my face, my voice, my stance, the way my name dances

      and slips right off the edge of any line I sign on.

QUEERING SUCCESS

You've   gone

        and   pulled

    yourself   up

        into   a   world

that doesn't   even want

            you.

because you were too lazy to put on makeup before you took your dog out for a walk. How could you be so foolish? You never leave the house without your armor. (Ugh, that metaphor. It's garbage, but so's this life.) This afternoon you make it exactly one half block from your front door before a group of men recognized you as something out-of-place. You're not sure what. You refuse to strain to interpret any gaze too small to hold you. All you know is the knife-sharp sensation of stare. And the muttering—*did you see that. what is that. hey you.* You shudder to give it voice. You want to place it in the bag with your dog's shit, but even her waste would spoil with their words. Fuck them. You keep on going. Every loud metal thing that passes by is a slow-motion meteor deciding whether or not it wants to head your way. You try your best to be inoffensive and correct— you force your shoulders down, push your cheeks up, narrow your eyes. You are prey scanning for predator while people happily water grass. They smile, they say hello, they don't want to kill you, you love them. When it is time to turn around and head back home, you prepare to once again meet the taunting men. You build a city for yourself inside your body in the moments it takes to clear their corner. You don't hang your head. You don't let anyone know your fear. You make it back alive, shut the door, and force yourself to leave the shades up until the sun begins to sink.

POEM

My mother loves the idea of me.

One afternoon, a tumbleweed
        the size of my body was
carried by hot wind
          into my path.

      Tiny golden stickers covered my surface
and hooked the flesh
        on my walk home from school.

I held my breath and pulled
        them out slowly in the bathroom
while she talked to her new boyfriend
          on the other side of the country.

He makes me happy, she says.
We're getting married, she says.

      I won't leave if you ask me not to leave, she says.
      I love you, I say. I rub my arms red.

The day she is meant to leave, I break
down and beg her not to leave and
she leaves.

THE BLUENESS OF THE ROOM

I stood in a freshly painted hall
and watched the moon

through the backdoor window.
Everything was bruise-colored and still.

Washing machine sounds drowned
out the rest of the house

and I felt myself become a trembling animal
in a way I could finally accept—

not like with you.
When I thought I heard your footsteps

in the kitchen, my head
snapped back like a rabbit's

and the moon was only a rock.
The blueness of the room a dream.

THE FRONT DOOR

A hungry dog inside her sternum screams when it opens.

She knows he is coming inside.
What she doesn't know, what she needs
more than food or air to know, is
what his problem will be.

What unspoken need has she failed to imagine this time?

What thorn, conjured
from the multiverse of wounded
would-be martyr-torsos,
will he pluck from his side
and jab her with today?

It is never not something—

be it dust on the counter,
the quiet way she asks for lunch money,
or just a girlish look in her eyes
he doesn't care for.

Reasons are butter to his rage—
he'll use the fake shit
as long as it keeps things cooking.

The foundation vibrates with his arrival.

She muzzles her heart.
She closes her door.
She crawls beneath her desk,
stays hungry.

GAME ANIMAL

I was murdered.
I was killed by a man.
I was strung up and gutted
over a blue plastic bucket.
As I died, I dreamt a vision
through my left eye:
I was walking along a cliff
near an ocean
full of pink and white water.
I climbed higher and higher,
but could not escape the rising tide.
The water kept laughing at me
even though I begged it not to.
When the spray hit me,
I leaned a little closer
as though I wanted to taste it.
All I wanted was to fall,
to disappear into the mouth
of something much larger than I.
But I kept on climbing
as the ground sighed like a
father's hand and squeezed.
Through my right eye,
I continued to watch my blood
gather and thicken beneath me.

JUSTIFICATION

He likes killing you after you're dead

—Tori Amos

It is what it is.

The knife

That carved

You up is

The knife

That taught you how

To avoid dropping

The knife

Onto your foot.

One could claim

The knife

Is what saved you

From

The knife

Itself.

TIME-LAPSE VIDEO OF TRANS WOMAN COLLAPSING INWARD LIKE A DYING STAR

I beg for invisible fire.

Every night I pray to love,
Please invent yourself.

I imagine a place after this place
and I laugh quietly to no one
as the hair on my chin
weeds through old makeup.

When I go to sleep
I am vinegar inside clouded glass.
The world comes to an end
when I wake up and wonder
who will be next to me.

Police sirens and coyote howls
blend together in morning's net.
Once, I walked out past the cars
and stood on a natural rock formation
that seemed placed there to be stood on.
I felt something like kinship.
It was the first time.

Once, I believed God
was a blanket of energy
stretched out around
our most vulnerable
places,

when really,

she's the sound
of a promise
breaking

GANGRENOUS LOVE

gangrenous love fills everything. a mind made blank
by careless hands turns purple in the sun. the fear

of closeness ripens. she had threatened to split her lips
open while the ocean made sounds in the distance.

every crashing wave gave water to the air as an
offering. the boys were off rolling blunts and laughing

too loud to hear all the violence. time stretches
and folds in on itself. time is a body full of damage

that is constantly trying to forget, though it always
remembers on the long drive home. the freeway is

such a beautiful trigger. machines like cold fruit
falling from city to city until one day they find

the soil. the same soil she moved her fingers through
when she thought of the love she gave away. the love

she held onto. all wrong, all backward, all pus-
covered memory. she slips into something more

comfortable, another reality. somewhere things are okay.
somewhere she is hacking off old limbs and dreaming

of velvety silence.

HOW MANY COLORS THERE ARE VS. HOW MANY COLORS HAVE BEEN NAMED

In this shadow
In this light
In this living body
I feel a spectrum.

How many feelings can one girl have?
That was a rhetorical question, I already know.

Everything goes on forever
long after we lose the ability
to process information.

When I appeared in the world for the first time
someone looked at my body
and said *boy*
and waved a pen like a magic wand.

Thirty years later I am lucky to have survived
all the deep reds and shining yellows
that surround this circle of gray.

We know the calm before the storm
can sometimes be the storm.

We have named almost nothing
and everything we have named
has been wrong.

TWO

AND THEN

CAME

THE NAMING

NEWSFEED

In the beginning, your name was Dying Girl.

Then, it became Public Debate.

You can't decide which has been worse.

The glow of their words

Reaches back behind your eyes

To make you know exactly

How they think you should live.

How they think you shouldn't live.

What you're supposed to be called after they've killed you.

POEM

you were born with beautiful hair and a body that could swim without thinking.

nothing else was necessary to say about you.

years later, you wished to be a slab of concrete next to a palm tree.
a freeway of thoughts begged you to end it all.
you circled above in the body of a hummingbird.

```
         *   *   *   *   *   *   *   *   *   *   *   *  * *  *
                  *                           *
     *   *                 * * * * * * DEATH
                        *              *
       *        WOMAN              *        *
                     HOOD* * *
       *              *                 *
                                     *
  *   *        *                   *        *
                            *
     *
          *     *        *     *     *       *    *    *   *
```

you used to spend all of your time looking at satellite and street-level views
of where you grew up. you needed to know it wasn't all a dream.

now, it's the only place you can remember.

you eat your fingers and imagine

branches growing from the stumps.

(you have no idea what kind of language doesn't exist
for who you are and what has happened)

HOUSEWIFE FROM PLANET X

*

She remembers where
  she comes from.

She wakes up in the body of a woman, the story of how
  she got here intact.

On Planet X, memory is not a part of the mind, but a chemical
  substance, like water.

When she sweats, she remembers. When she drinks, she
  remembers.

When she breathes warm air and exhales cold mist into her
  hands, she remembers.

There is no word on Planet X that signifies forgetting.

*

She was born a roll of paper
towels. The more pieces of her body
you'd tear off, the more of her there would be.

*

Violence is the scroll upon which her history is recorded.

They called her a boy
even when they pushed her head down the toilet
even when she built a glove from her fingernail clippings
and clawed her way
out

*

I don't want to be understood

.

*

I remember

*

I died and came back I don't want you to believe in me or celebrate

*

*

*

remember

*

Her Survival:

Keep all corners clean. Don't miss a single spot.
Dust is death. Dust is death. Dust is death.

Paint a perfect scene and be the sun in the corner.
Hold your hidden planet in place.

Warm everything but yourself.
Burn off the parts of you that offend.

All of you offends.
Burn off all of you.

*

She wakes up the day of her wedding
Half human and dehydrated.

She shaves her face.
She tucks.
She forgets.

POEM

Bliss is where I was never touched. Bliss is a dreamheaven projected through my eyelids against a screen made from gigantic yellow leaves. Fatherless, I have never danced harder, shined louder. Motherless, I am dead but make my final breath a forever songdream for any soul on the verge of green-speckled hell who wants to hold my lonely voice for however long it will allow your grasp.

COERCION ROAD

The first time it happened, we had just seen a dead body on the side of the highway. It was February 13th. When we arrived at the hotel room, I looked up the news and found out the body belonged to a woman who'd tossed herself in front of a passing truck. I couldn't shake the image of her lying on her back in the middle of the road between police cars, her broken face pushed out from beneath the white sheet, eyeless. You began to climb and lick me and I kept saying, *No, please, I can't stop seeing for her.* From that day forward, I dreamt of hot asphalt beneath my bare back every time I was shoved into a bed and told to be anything I wasn't.

A CONFESSION

The day the government announced another plan to strip a few
more basic rights from trans people, I had sex with someone I
met via Tinder. I'd been rejected that afternoon by another who'd
referred to me as *so beautiful*, but unmatched when I informed
her of my gender situation. The person I ended up meeting, on
the other hand, was cool with it. So cool, she let me know in the
middle of fucking she had *kind of a thing for chicks with
dicks*. She called me *the best of both worlds*, and smiled, as
though she were the first person to think or say that. I promised
myself I would process this another time. As she rode me she said
she was pretending my dick was hers, that she was using it on
me. Reader, I was extremely into this. I was even more into it
when she flipped me over and starting grinding herself against
my ass. *Oh my God I'm gonna cum*, she moaned and I felt her
warmth trickle down my crack and soak my little hole and I could
hardly stay inside my body. Afterward, I snuggled my head
against her chest while she spoke of a desire to explore her
masculine side, thanking me for giving her the chance to express
it. I ran my fingers through her closely cropped hair, stroking the
little buzz of sideburn next to her gorgeous, metal-adorned ear. I
see it, I said, tilting my face to meet her gaze. *I see you.* She
pulled me closer into her arms and sighed against the back of my
neck. Later, while saliva dripped from above onto my waiting
tongue, I wondered what it would mean to see myself. What I
might be. When I was finished swallowing her spit, I went to say
something, but she didn't notice. *You're beautiful*, was all she
could repeat. *So beautiful.*

A CONFESSION

There's a door marked: *Come lie*
your head in a stranger's
lap and have her play with your hair
while reminding you over and over why you deserve to live.

The only problem, and you know this, you know it,
is whenever you touch the door handle
the floor opens beneath you, and
you fall

for what feels like days or years or seconds.
You're surrounded by white light
and can't make anything out
except everything

around you.
You become the light. You drown yourself
out. You sit through hours of conversation
with someone who thinks you're beautiful

and isn't afraid to tell you.
She leans into your void, as if to kiss,
as if to drink. Once she has had a sip or two,
she'll say something like

Wow. I can't believe you used to be a man.
I literally would have never known.
No one would have ever guessed unless
they used an electron microscope on your

voice. You repeat her words back to yourself
as love. It's not long
until you're in a bed, still falling.

Once she has taken plenty of gulps from you,
you are ready for sleep, for death.
But gold wire surrounds
your center

pulling you up up up up, past bars and
freeways and houses
you can make out so much better than
your own body.

By the time you're through the floor,
through the door, and she is holding you,
whispering sand-filled honey, soothing you
to sleep,

you'll have forgotten what you look like or
        who you belong to.

CHILDHOOD PRAYER

(God,   Kiss me

    Goodnight and   Take me away from here.

I am a cactus when   I was supposed to be

    The water inside the cactus.   Bring me into your glow

Where I can feel enclosed,   And let me be swallowed

    Without ever being   Touched—drink from me quietly,

Beneath starlight   Where I belong.)

ESPINOZA:

A name whose meaning has
something to do with thorns.

The origins are disputed
but that much

               the thorns

is clear.

             All I know is
             I've been storing all this water
                far too long.

Maybe I need to
finally embrace
the power of language

and say what needs to be said
about what has happened here.

             Maybe
             in the next poem.

POEM

This isn't a poem. I don't write poems anymore. Poems are where I used to hide parts of myself I was afraid of, so they couldn't touch me, couldn't remind me that I am not a poem but a woman, not a woman but a victim, not a victim but a hummingbird, not a hummingbird but a nest, not a nest but a window reflection of a tree catching the last gasp of this afternoon's breeze. A long time ago I decided I'd let the wind take me wherever it wanted to take me even though I am surrounded on all four sides by concrete. This is how I became a living vortex of paper and pine needles outside your door. This is how I became a poem. I beat my body against the walls long enough that they began to give. And you heard my screaming. And you screamed back. And we were together. Once we finish rescuing me, I'll have nothing to say unless it is entirely clear and perfect and inseparable from my flesh. The poem the idea the self the poem the idea the self the poem the idea the self the poem the idea the self the poem the idea the self

RESURRECTION

My mother set my body on fire.
She had to hide the evidence.

She didn't understand what she was doing.
At least, that is what I tell myself

when I spend afternoons with her,
and her trans ally tattoo, and her refusal

to speak about anything but an imagined past—
as though ash could be willed back into daughter.

LOSS RITUAL

This one involves stretching
the skin until it begins to break.

There is light that escapes, and
light that enters. We call this

an even trade, but I am still
without family. Poured myself

a glass of womanhood and drank
until the bones became enough

to live in. Said you can have this
old thing. I don't need it anymore.

Lick the salt from its surface. I
don't need it anymore. I can cry

whenever I want, all it takes is
remembering. You wanted to

be holy and righteous because
this is one path to one kind

of heaven. I wanted to be holy
and righteous because life is short

and sad and we all deserve to be
loved. Even you, alone with your

God. Even me, alone with myself.
Neither as complete as we hoped

the loss would make us.

AIRPORT RITUAL

I go to the airport to get on an airplane to see my family.

<u>I am not afraid</u>
I pretend my body is not part of my narrative.

<u>I am not afraid</u>
I get scanned by the body scanner.

<u>I am not afraid</u>
My anomaly is unspotted.

<u>I am not afraid</u>
I pass through unscathed, this time.

<u>I am not afraid</u>
I pretend being scanned by the body scanner is not part of my narrative.

<u>I am not afraid</u>
Even when I cry in the bathroom,

<u>I am not afraid</u>
Changing out of too-tight shapewear

<u>I am not afraid</u>
Holding all of me in place.

<u>I am not afraid</u>

<u>I am not afraid</u>

<u>I am not afraid</u>

<u>I am not afraid</u>

<u>I am not afraid</u>

<u>I am not afraid</u>
My body is not part of my narrative.

<u>I am not afraid</u>
This is helpful to remember when I get on the airplane.

<u>I am not afraid</u>
I am going to see my family,

<u>I am not afraid</u>
Many of whom have not spoken to me since

<u>I am not afraid</u>
I started calling myself Jennifer.

<u>I am not afraid</u>
I order a vodka tonic (*two shots, please*) and show my ID.

<u>I am not afraid</u>
Nothing bad happens.

<u>I am not afraid</u>
My name matches my face matches my body.

<u>I am not afraid</u>
Fear is no longer a part of my narrative.

<u>I am not afraid</u>
I understand my place in the plot of things.

<u>I am not afraid</u>
The plane lands and I go to my family,

<u>I am not afraid</u>
My body no longer a part of my narrative.

NORMAL

is fucked and impossible
for me to take. It was normal
for my body to be pummeled
until it called itself a boy.
It was normal to die.
It was normal for the news
to question whether or not
I exist. It was normal
for the blood I came from
to rebuke me in the name of God.
It was normal for people to wave God
like a spinning helicopter blade
over the wild heads of
faggots such as I.
It was normal
to stay indoors and die.
It was normal to be reborn.
It was normal to be trampled
by trained elephants.
It was normal to forgive.
It was normal to not forgive
myself. It was normal
to pray for thrombosis.
It was normal to not
taste the sun and
it was normal to have good
reason to be afraid to.

REAL WOMAN

A woman can look like anything.
I was not alive until
I tried to understand this.

     When I was a girl, I appeared as
     a December hillside
     whose snow settled in places too low.

          I weathered the beat
          of protesting wind against
          my clothing as long as I could.

               I skipped lunches,
               forged permission slips,
               wiped makeup off in the car after school,

          held space
          for everybody's grievances
          with my body.

     When I grew scared of becoming an avalanche,
     I tore off my face
     and birthed a river.

A woman can look like anything,
I laughed, buzzing
what was left of my head

                    down the sink.

WHERE AND WHAT I AM

When I sit on the couch,   I fall into snow.
When I picture snow,   I become a raven.
In bed,   I am twelve.
In the shower,   I've just turned five.
In a warm breeze,   I am eight.
In a cool breeze,   I am four.

There is never not a ringing in my ears.
It is how I know I am always me.

In November,   I am sixteen and ten
                                  and a thirty-two-year-old woman
                                  who won't be stopped.

In March,   I am a baby.
For one moment in the middle of July,   I cease to exist.
When I'm reborn,   I appear in the form of fresh-cut grass.

I'm bagged and trashed
before I learn how to say—.

When the right person kisses me,   I am a ticking clock.
When the wrong person touches me,   I am a broken videotape.

In the morning,   I am two and a half years old.
In the afternoon,   I am one and three quarters.
In the evening,   I am moments away from my own
demise.

I gather everyone in me
and spin us in circles around the kitchen
until we remember the way we share

this body;   this unbalance.

WE

Dreams rain.

Digs down deep, not to hide, but to excavate.

Kisses blood.

Trusts the pulse.

Never holds its fingers to its wrists for anything.

Moves like waves.

Moves like fog.

Moves like breathing.

Knows the end is coming if it wants.

Pushes into.

Crawls out of.

Blooms fist into open hand.

Shatters hand into mess of bone and flesh and flowers.

Grips the bad man's mouth, points it up at sky.

Considers this a great mercy.

Travels to a hillside where nothing but rock grows.

Pulls apart the rocks.

Breaks them with bare fingers.

Removes spines.

Removes seeds.

Removes heart.

Sprouts thousands of cacti from base to peak.

Summons the always-late light of the sun.

Turns shadows solid while earth becomes memory.

Draws up plans to will this place into something survivable.

HOW I MAKE A POEM

Rhetoric I steal from men who hurt me.
Wisdom I take from a God I ghosted.

I feeling through thread.
I forge name and social.

I spit into goldshine.
I dream water and drink

roomfuls of flowers
roomfuls of flowers

roomfuls of flowers
roomfuls of flowers.

In this poem I learn how to kiss.
In this poem I learn how to be touched.

In this poem I fuck without reeling.
I truth with my body until I disappears.

YOUR WEAKNESS

Air
against
    your skin
is a trigger.
Regardless,
    you go
about your day.
You read,
    write,
        teach,
            cook,
                sing,
                    take care
                        of a dog
                            even more
                                fucked up
                                    than
                                        you are.
                                    You love her
                                    with all of
                                    your being.
                                You love singing,
                                cooking,
                            teaching,
                        writing,
                    reading,
                the way
            every
        movement
of
yours
    feels
        like an
            act of war

against this

    earth.

       There

          is infinite

            power

               in your

                  so-called

                     weakness.

TODAY I WAS ALONE

Today I was alone, confident, and full
of grace. I thought of something you
once told me—*to be alive is to win*

a fight. I know this is true because
I left the house and talked to others
and made lunch for myself. For a moment

my breathing was in question,
but the hills and the sidewalk and
the view of the city reminded me what

was at stake. This is a world of pieces.
In it I am five, maybe six, things out
of infinity. I am able to enter my feet

and say *walk.* I can even go into
my hands and tell them to relax.
Everyone acts like a tree is what you

see above the ground. They think
all these freeways came from nowhere.
No one sees all the invisible work I do

to avoid the daily violence of cohesion.
Of saying *we are all human* with no
further movement toward it. I stay

in place, play up my laziness and
call it a radical gesture. I love this space
I've built for my hope. Freedom only

exists in its dream of itself—a haunted
hallway you pull me down with a smile
as though you knew I was going to make it.

I TALKED TO THAT SPIRIT AGAIN

I talked to that spirit again
the one who says I deserve
goodness and joy and the

daily sight of women burning
down parking garages. She says
there is a harmony between

nature and artifice, that we simply
need to find new ways to introduce
them to each other. So I wrap my

head in freshly plucked leaves and
jump through the window.
The broken glass becomes a

blessing upon the earth. I see
myself as nothing more than a scar
against its surface, a rough daydream

of healing. The spirit says I am wrong,
that I am the world denied by the
world, the language rejected

by the tongue. I tell her the time
for debate is over—
all that is left is for me to sink

back into myself and kiss and hold
every beloved soul who wipes the
blood from my eyes and

calls me by my true name.

THIS IS WHAT MAKES US WORLDS

Like light but
in reverse we billow.

We turn a corner
and make the hills
disappear.

You rearrange
my parts until no
more hurting.

No more skin-sunk
nighttime fear.

No more blameless death.

My hair loses its atoms.
My body glows
in the dark.

Planets are smashed
into oblivion,
stripped of their power
to name things.

Our love fills the air.

Our love eats
the deadly sounds men
make when they see
how much magic
we have away
from them.

MEMOIR

Wherever you were, you didn't want to be there.
You finally taught yourself how to say no.
It happened just yesterday
inside your nesting's spiny subsurface.
You crawled out bloody
possibly victorious
having refused the somatic argument
that spreads its seed
through the winds of your womanly thrashing.
Some days you're wild enough
to sit still and hold pain's hand
until your flesh becomes its glove
and not the other way around.
Regardless, remembering is what moves you.
Your first backyard arrived as dirt
before becoming patches
of overgrown weeds and grass.
You never said a thing there
until you were told.
This morning's garden began as grass
and transformed into a red planet
of peppers and spiderwebs and dirt.
You don't say shit here unless you feel like it.

THE PRESENT

When I arrive
the fig tree in the yard
will rain its fruit upon my body
while somebody beautiful watches
and films me
and plays the footage back
while telling me
I am also beautiful
without using any words.

I cannot believe I am alive.

I
really
pulled
it
off.

I
am going wild with crush
on my throat's
hard-won nature.

For a lifetime, sensation was
a single thread
in my wardrobe of pain.

It formed the big white curtain
through which I fought to view
the green of my garden.

That I am not dead now
is how I know exactly two things:

I have bathed my leaves in a dark-lit love.

I have fucked with the fabric of time in order to exist.

BY THE CEMETERY ON PINE

You are real, I reminded myself one day.
I ran this idea up a kite string and pulled it

through the warm air of the nearest park.
Sprinting, toes in grass turning yellow-green,

I looked up to find my paper-thin faith gone,
my string still flying, held in place by a bit of sky.

BIOGRAPHY OF A SNOWSTORM

Sources say you were born in a bright
patch next to a busy freeway.

Others claim a cloud came to life
and swooped you up without a word.

Someone else told me the sound of your own
scream was enough to finish you off.

This is what I know for certain:

It is the end of your life every day. You are two
years old and dancing on carpet, surrounded
by woods. Mountain air is your father.
Your mother has disappeared.   She is holding you.

There is a light in the sky.
It sings behind your closet door.
It crawls into your mouth at night.

It says, *Look at*
          the snow.

Isn't it
beautiful?

Your body is a sleeping bag packed with snow.
You die and go to heaven and it is a fireplace full of snow.
You come back to life and make a snow angel in your own ashes.

Multiple witnesses tell me you lived through one hell of an avalanche,
though historical records fail to indicate the existence of any such event.

ADDENDUM

this is how i became a poet: i was a baby. the snow fell. i was alone. i watched it.

this is how i became a poet: i left my body one night while static played on television.

this is how i became a poet: an orange light was hurting me.

this is how i became a poet: i learned to stare at a wall until i became its daughter.

this is how i became a poet: my pillow was the savings account where i stored my
        screams when i couldn't afford the relief of unobstructed expression.

this is how i became a poet: i built a spaceship out of blankets, chairs, parts of a
        broken bed.

this is how i became a poet: i lived an entire life as a broken bed.

this is how i became a poet: i learned to lucid dream my way into another world.

this is how i became a poet: i took all the hurt i was asked to carry and heal, both
        mine and that of others, and i dropped it off the edge of a cliff after tying
        it all by rope to my tongue.

this is how i became a poet: i danced in the blood.

this is how i became a poet: i forgot my past and then remembered all of it at once
        the day my first book was published and had a body-quaking panic
        attack that lasted over twelve hours but released none of the horror. so i
        wrote a second book.

this is how i became a poet: i kicked my name apart with love.

this is how i became a poet: i spent years sleeping in my mother's childhood
        bedroom.

this is how i became a poet: i billowed around an old garage occupied by boxes full
        of family.

this is how i became a poet: i became who i was and was abandoned by my family.

this is how i became a poet: i witnessed the air spend all its time trying to convince
        me to accept it.

this is how i became a poet: i made myself fight exceptionally hard to love me.

DEPARTURE

*

An anomaly is spotted.

[*i am going to have to touch you now*]
an agent says.

[*i am going to use the front of my hands on most of you, will use
the backs of my hands on places that are private.*   *is there
anything you need to tell me before i proceed?*]

I lean in and whisper,
I'm trans
as a warning or apology or both.

[*would you like to take this somewhere more private?*] she asks.

Without thinking, I answer, *No.*

I wonder if I just want to get it over with
as quickly as possible
or maybe
I desire an uncovering—
to force the other passengers to watch
my right leg quake
as the agent's hands become machinery
scanning up and down my length.

*

[*you have such thick, beautiful hair*]
the agent says from behind
in a smileless tone
as she runs blue latex

through its strands
during a second
unexpected
even more intrusive searching.

I watch white dads in red baseball hats watch us and I wonder.

In this place, I am always so full of wonder.

The agent tells me I'm clear,
and to have a good day.
I say, *Thank you*
but not in the usual
honey-soaked, performative
polite voice
I use for strangers
and family.

*

A day earlier
at a family wedding
my aunt approached.

She took a hug and said it was great to see me.

The last time she reached out,
five years ago
Christmas morning
her words were something like:

[*don't come*

over unless

               you arrive

in the form of a

man. i don't want

my kids to know you.   ]

I loved my cousins. I missed their lives.

I pulled away from her hug and said
it was great to see her too
in a tone I never knew I carried.

Neither sarcastic nor bitchy; simply flat. Emotion-free.
The way taking a breath feels when you want to die
but don't.

I was proud of myself for not shrinking
like I usually do
in response to unwanted touch.

*

I use the same voice with the agent when I tell her, *Thank you.*

I walk to the bathroom and
don't let anyone
see me cry.

IT DOESN'T MATTER IF I'M UNDERSTOOD

You'll still try to destroy me in your own way

Maybe with your hands
Maybe with your silence
Maybe with your tacit approval of this machine

Here us women are
crackling like sparklers above a lawn
scraping diamonds from asphalt
giving praise to the mountains before us

Our love and our grace and our tenderness
enough to change the shape of the universe

You say *Goddess* or you say *dead girl*
We live in the margins but don't get a taste
of the joy of being there

Not without loss
Not without broken bones and bandaged flesh

Our condition is nameless
and we know this
so we drift and deflate and let the wind have us

but we don't stop living
even when we sense our impending ghost
even when we finger the dirt and think home

Our life was always a thing of magic
and magic is what lives outside of law

One day we will be allowed to exist
and you will never see us again

I don't want to be understood— I don't want to be understood— want to live in the air understood— want to live in the

I want to live in the air with all my sisters floating free around me with all my sisters floating free around me

like dandelion seeds No blood like dandelion seeds No blood

No language

No speaking

No border between

Just feeling Pure feeling

One day she will fall in love

all along

all along

all along

where she realized all along we've been touching beneath the soil

all along

all along

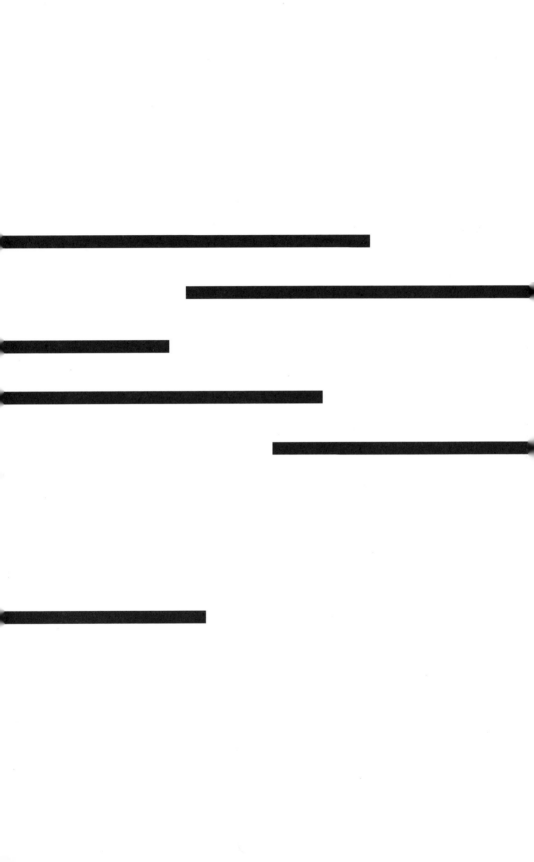

ACKNOWLEDGMENTS

Poems in this book have been featured in *The American Poetry Review*, *Anomaly*, *BOAAT Journal*, *Granta*, *POETRY*, *Poem-a-Day* at Poets.org, *Spiral Orb*, Split This Rock's *The Quarry: A Social Justice Poetry Database*, *Them*, *VIDA Review*, and *West Branch*; in addition, some of these poems have been anthologized in *Set Me On Fire: A Poem For Every Feeling* (Doubleday/Penguin Random House), *Subject to Change: Trans Poetry & Conversation* (Sibling Rivalry Press), and *We Want It All: An Anthology of Radical Trans Poetics* (Nightboat Books).

RECENT TITLES FROM ALICE JAMES BOOKS

Canandaigua, Donald Revell

In the Days That Followed, Kevin Goodan

Light Me Down: The New & Collected Poems of Jean Valentine, Jean Valentine

Song of My Softening, Omotara James

Theophanies, Sarah Ghazal Ali

Orders of Service, Willie Lee Kinard III

The Dead Peasant's Handbook, Brian Turner

The Goodbye World Poem, Brian Turner

The Wild Delight of Wild Things, Brian Turner

I Am the Most Dangerous Thing, Candace Williams

Burning Like Her Own Planet, Vandana Khanna

Standing in the Forest of Being Alive, Katie Farris

Feast, Ina Cariño

Decade of the Brain: Poems, Janine Joseph

American Treasure, Jill McDonough

We Borrowed Gentleness, J. Estanislao Lopez

Brother Sleep, Aldo Amparán

Sugar Work, Katie Marya

Museum of Objects Burned by the Souls in Purgatory, Jeffrey Thomson

Constellation Route, Matthew Olzmann

How to Not Be Afraid of Everything, Jane Wong

Brocken Spectre, Jacques J. Rancourt

No Ruined Stone, Shara McCallum

The Vault, Andrés Cerpa

White Campion, Donald Revell

Last Days, Tamiko Beyer

If This Is the Age We End Discovery, Rosebud Ben-Oni

Pretty Tripwire, Alessandra Lynch

Inheritance, Taylor Johnson

The Voice of Sheila Chandra, Kazim Ali

Arrow, Sumita Chakraborty

Country, Living, Ira Sadoff

Hot with the Bad Things, Lucia LoTempio

Witch, Philip Matthews

Alice James Books is committed to publishing books that matter. The press was founded in 1973 in Boston, Massachusetts to give women access to publishing. As a cooperative, authors performed the day-to-day undertakings of the press. The press continues to expand and grow from its formative roots, guided by its founding values of access, excellence, inclusivity, and collaboration in publishing. Its mission is to publish books that matter and preserve a place of belonging for poets who inspire us. AJB seeks to broaden our collective interpretation of what constitutes the American poetic voice and is dedicated to helping its artists achieve purposeful engagement with broad audiences and communities nationwide. The press was named for Alice James, sister to William and Henry, whose extraordinary gift for writing went unrecognized during her lifetime.

Designed by Tiani Kennedy

Printed by Sheridan Saline